PET OWNER'S GUIDE TO THE
HAMSTER

Lorraine Hill

RINGPRESS

ABOUT THE AUTHOR

Lorraine Hill has kept hamsters for many years – both Syrian and Dwarf – and has specialised in breeding and exhibiting them. She has written numerous articles on hamsters, and has contributed to material published by the British Hamster Association, the Heart of England Hamster Club and the Southern Hamster Club. She has also produced a web-site entitled The Complete Hamster Site, which has provoked much interest both in the UK and overseas. Lorraine is a highly-skilled photographer of small animals, and she has provided most of the illustrations for this book.

ACKNOWLEDGEMENTS

Many thanks to Chris Henwood, and grateful acknowledgements to the late Roy Robinson and the late Bob Parlett, who have all shared so much knowledge with me over the years of keeping hamsters. Thanks also to my hamsters, and to those of my friends, for posing for photographs, and to the handlers in the photos – Clare Everitt, Majed Sabir and Emma Friend. Thanks to the Angel Aquarium Pet Shop, Didcot, and the Marcham Pet Store near Abingdon, for allowing me to create chaos while taking photographs. Finally, my thanks to Amanda Bulbeck for providing additional photography.

DEDICATION

I would like to dedicate this book to my very good friend Joanna Roach, whom I met many years ago through our mutual love of hamsters, and who has given me so much encouragement in writing this book.

Published by Ringpress Books Limited,
PO Box 8, Lydney, Gloucestershire,
GL15 6YD, United Kingdom.

First published 1998
©1998 Ringpress Books Limited. All rights reserved

ISBN 1 86054 0538

CONTENTS

INTRODUCING THE HAMSTER 6

History (Syrian Hamster; Dwarf Campbells Russian Hamster; Dwarf Winter White Russian Hamster; Chinese Hamster; Roborovski Hamster); Hamster fancy; Choosing a hamster; Different varieties; Where to buy a hamster; The right type; Male or female?; How many?; A healthy hamster; Sexing hamsters.

THE RIGHT START 17

Hamster cages (Basic cages; Multi-level cages; Aquariums; Home-made cages); Wood shavings; Nesting material; Food bowl; Drinking bottle; Hamster wheels; Hamster balls; Furnishing the cage; Play areas; Travelling boxes; Feeding; Hamster mix; Green food; Hamster treats; Quantity; Bran/oat mash: Water

CARING FOR YOUR HAMSTER 27

Settling in; General care; Cleaning the cage; Grooming; Handling your hamster; Running loose; Levels of response; Additional checks; Hamster behaviour; Escapes and captures.

SPECIES AND COLOURS 37

Syrian Hamster (Colours; Patterns; Coat types); Dwarf Campbells Russian Hamster (Colours; Patterns; Coat types); Dwarf Winter White Russian Hamster (Colours; Patterns); Chinese Hamster (Colours; Patterns); Roborovski Hamster (Colours).

5 BREEDING HAMSTERS 53

Making the decision; The right age; The right condition; Mating (Syrian Hamster; Dwarf Hamsters); The Pregnant Hamster (Syrian Hamster; Dwarf Hamster); Preparations; The birth; Inspecting the litter; Caring for the litter; Weaning.

6 SHOWING HAMSTERS 66

Getting ready; At the show; Judging procedure.

7 HEALTH CARE 74

Colds; Diarrhoea; Constipation; Wet Tail; Mites; Cuts and wounds; Hibernation; Overgrown/chipped teeth; Broken limbs; Shock; Strokes; Fur loss; Brain tumours; Cancers/tumours; Long nails; Eyeless hamsters; Loss of limb.

1

Introducing The Hamster

Hamsters belong to the rodent family and are so called because of their habit of hoarding food – the word 'hamster' is derived from the German word 'hamstern', meaning 'to hoard'. They are nocturnal by nature and in the wild they live in burrows consisting of tunnels and chambers. They avoid the heat of the day by sleeping in their burrows, and foraging for food during the cooler evenings and nights. Most species of hamster have expandable cheekpouches in which they can collect and carry food and bedding, and they may travel many miles collecting food each night, returning to their burrows and emptying it into their food store. Some species of hamster, such as the Syrian Hamster, can carry up to half their body weight in food in their cheekpouches.

There are 27 species and sub-species of hamster found in different countries and habitats,

with the majority living in semi-desert areas, but not all are kept as pets. The species most commonly kept as pets are, in descending order, the Syrian Hamster (Mesocricetus Auratus), sometimes referred to as the Golden (short-haired) or Teddybear (long-haired) Hamster; the Dwarf Campbells Russian Hamster (Phodopus Sungoris Campbelli); the Dwarf Winter White Russian Hamster (Phodopus Sungoris Sungoris), sometimes referred to as the Djungarian or Siberian Hamster; the Chinese Hamster (Cricetulus Griseus), and the Roborovski Hamster (Phodopus Roborovskii).

HISTORY
Syrian Hamster:
The Syrian Hamster originates from the desert areas of Syria and was first recorded by George Waterhouse, Curator of the London Zoological Society, when he presented the 'new' species to

The Syrian Hamsters are named after the habit of hoarding food.

the Society in 1839. It is known to have been kept in the UK from 1880 until 1910. Syrian Hamsters were not seen in the wild for some time and were thought to be extinct until a female Syrian Hamster and her young were captured at Aleppo, Syria, in 1930 by Dr Israel Aharoni, a zoologist, and taken to the Hebrew University, Jerusalem.

Some of these were bred and their descendants were later imported into the UK and the USA and used in laboratories. Staff working in the laboratories realised what wonderful pets these hamsters would make, and the Syrian Hamster was introduced to the pet market in 1945. Since this time, many coat and colour mutations have occurred and the Syrian Hamster now exists in a variety of colours. Wild captures have been made since 1930 in the Aleppo area of Syria, but it is not

Black Eyed Cream Syrian

clear whether any of these hamsters were bred from. The Syrian Hamster is now widely kept in captivity but is rare, if not extinct, in the wild.

Dwarf Campbells Russian:
The Dwarf Campbells Russian originates from Central Asia, Northern Russia and North China and lives among the sand dunes. It has been kept in the UK since 1963, was introduced to the UK pet market in the 1970s and is now available on the pet market in many countries. These are the

INTRODUCING THE HAMSTER

Russian Hamsters most often seen in pet stores. Some colour mutations have occurred both in captivity and in the wild.

Dwarf Winter White Russian:
The Dwarf Winter White Russian originates from the grassy steppes of eastern Kazakhstan and south west Siberia, was introduced into the UK pet market in 1978 and is now available on the pet market in many countries. It is called Winter White because during the winter months, when the number of daylight hours are reduced, the coat turns white, which serves as camouflage in the snow against predators in its natural environment. These hamsters are not as commonly seen as the Dwarf Campbells Russian Hamster, and have fewer colour mutations at present.

Chinese: The Chinese Hamster originates from Northern China and Mongolia and belongs to a group known as rat-like hamsters. The Chinese Hamster has been kept in the UK since 1919 but was not widely kept in laboratories. Interest in Chinese Hamsters grew in the 1970s following the introduction of the Russian Hamster to the pet market, although, because of their mouse-like appearance, they do not share the popularity of the Russian Hamsters. The Chinese Hamster is available on the pet market in many countries today.

Roborovski:
The Roborovski Hamster originates from sandy desert areas of Mongolia and Northern China. It was kept by London Zoo in the 1960s, but the present UK stock was imported from Holland in 1990. These Hamsters are still relatively rare as pets and are not readily available on the pet market, but are kept by specialised breeders in a few countries.

HAMSTER FANCY
As hamsters became popular pets and were bred by enthusiasts, the first UK hamster club (the British Hamster Club) was formed in the 1940s. This was followed by the formation of regional clubs. As colour mutations started to occur, hamster enthusiasts started to breed and maintain these new mutations. The clubs catered only for Syrian Hamsters and, although Dwarf Hamsters were introduced to the pet market in the 1970s, it was not until the 1980s that the UK hamster clubs began to cater for owners of Dwarf Hamsters and allow them to be shown.

Today, all UK hamster clubs cater for Syrian and Dwarf Hamsters, and there are at least six clubs specifically designed for hamster owners and two governing bodies – the British Hamster Association and the National Hamster Council. Hamster clubs now also exist in Sweden, Finland, Holland and many countries have rodent or pet clubs which cater for hamster owners.

CHOOSING A HAMSTER

It should be remembered that any pet is a living creature and will need care, time and attention. Hamsters are very popular as pets in many countries for children and adults alike. They are relatively easy to keep, take up little time, cost very little to keep and take up very little room, making them an ideal pet for those living in a small apartment, or those at school or working during the day, as they will easily fit into any household routine.

Hamsters are clean animals, washing themselves and having

Platinum Dwarf Campbells Russian: These are lively, and may be quick to nip if anr.

INTRODUCING THE HAMSTER

Sapphire Winter White Russian.

very little or no smell, even designating one area of the cage as a toilet area. They are nocturnal and their eyesight is poor, so they rely mainly on smell and hearing. They are lively, agile, friendly and good climbers, and can provide hours of amusement.

DIFFERENT VARIETIES

The Syrian Hamster is a suitable pet for children and adults alike. It is big enough to be handled by small children, but care should be taken that it is not squeezed by young hands, which could cause the hamster to nip, become frightened or hurt. The typical size of a Syrian Hamster is 15-20 cm, with females being larger than males. The average lifespan is $2-2^{1}/_{2}$ years, but they can live longer – up to 4 years is not unknown.

Dwarf Campbells Russian Hamsters and Dwarf Winter White Russian Hamsters are more suited to older children or adults because of their lively nature and small size. They are not so easily handled by small children and can be a little more quick to nip if annoyed than the Syrian Hamster. The typical size of a Campbells

Dominant Spot Chinese: These hamsters will live together in harmony.

Russian is 10-12 cm and the Winter White Russian 8-10 cm with males being larger than females. The average lifespan is $1^1/_2$-2 years but they can live longer, and some have been known to live until 4 years of age.

The Chinese Hamster, although not technically a dwarf hamster, is around 10-12 cm in length, with males being larger than females. It is, again, better suited to older children or adults. They can be fast moving but very quiet to handle and generally good natured. The average lifespan is $1^1/_2$-2 years, but they can live longer.

The Roborovski Hamster is extremely lively and the smallest of the dwarf hamsters, being typically 4-5 cm in length. Because of its extremely lively nature it is not a pet to be handled easily by children or adults, but is rather one to be observed. However, if handled they are very tame, although very lively! The average lifespan is unclear at present but they seem to be longer-lived than the other dwarf hamsters.

WHERE TO BUY A HAMSTER

The best place to buy a hamster, without doubt, is from a reputable breeder. Hamster clubs may know of and be able to put you in touch with breeders in your area. Alternatively, private breeders may advertise hamsters for sale locally on shop noticeboards or in local papers. Buying a hamster direct from the breeder enables you to see the parents and find out the exact date of birth of the hamster, its diet and its likes and dislikes. Many pet stores sell hamsters, but do not usually have the wide range of colours or varieties available from private breeders. For most the pet store is the most likely place to obtain their first hamster. Ensure that, if buying a hamster from a pet store, they are housed in clean and adequate conditions, the condition of the hamsters appears good and males and females are housed separately.

THE RIGHT TYPE

One of the most important factors to take into account when buying a hamster is the age of the owner, and the number of hamsters required. The Syrian Hamster is a solitary animal, and once it has reached maturity will not usually tolerate the company of another.

Therefore, if more than one hamster is required but you do not wish to purchase more than

The Robrovski is kept by specialised breeders.

Choose a young hamster that appears healthy and inquisitive.

one cage, a Dwarf Hamster is the answer. Dwarf Hamsters are social hamsters and will live happily together in single sex or mixed sex pairs or groups. Obviously, mixed sex pairs or groups will breed.

If you require a pet to handle, then the Syrian, Dwarf Campbells Russians, Dwarf Winter White Russian or the Chinese is suitable, but if you want an interesting pet to observe, the Roborovski is the choice for you.

MALE OR FEMALE?

Males are generally more even-tempered than females, although with regular handling any hamster will become tame. However, if buying Dwarf Hamsters to be kept together in a single sex group or pair, males generally settle better together than females.

HOW MANY?

As mentioned above, Syrian Hamsters must have a cage of their own and so two hamsters means two cages will be required. Dwarf Hamsters (Campbells Russian, Winter White Russian, Chinese, Roborovski) can be kept in either mixed or single sex groups or pairs, and as a general rule pairs or groups should be housed in a cage that allows a space of at least 60 sq cm per hamster. Dwarf Hamsters are better kept in pairs or groups rather than singly, as they are sociable animals and to keep one on its own is considered stressful to the hamster and may shorten its lifespan.

A HEALTHY HAMSTER

It is important when selecting a hamster that different sexes are housed in different cages. Hamsters can breed at a very young age and buying a female hamster from a cage where male

and females are housed together could mean buying a pregnant female.

1. AGE:

A hamster should not be sold under five weeks of age, and the ideal age to buy a hamster is between five and ten weeks of age.

2. BEHAVIOUR:

You should look for a hamster that is alert and inquisitive when awake but not too nervous.

3. HEALTH:

Check underneath and around the tail to see that there is no wetness which could be a sign of

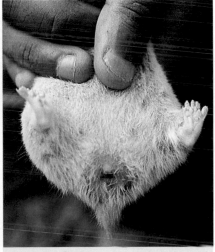

A female Syrian.

A male Syrian.

Black Tortoiseshell Syrian

diarrhoea. Check the coat is clean, the body is firm, the eyes are ears are clean and that the hamster has no obvious signs of illness – running nose, discharge or sneezing.

4. TEMPERAMENT:

Ask if you can handle the hamster that appeals to you so that you can assess its temperament and suitability as a pet.

SEXING HAMSTERS

The breeder or pet store should be able to check the sex of your chosen hamster. The principal of sexing any hamster is the same – hold the hamster with one hand over the body and the other underneath its belly and turn the hamster over to look at the genitals. Alternatively, hold the hamster by the scruff of the neck to look at the genitals.

On the female, the vaginal opening is very close to the anus – sometime so close that it is difficult to distinguish the two separate vents. On the male, there is a gap between the penile opening and the anus – this gap can be 1 cm or so on Dwarf Hamsters and 2 cm or more on Syrian Hamsters. The rear end is also more elongated and bulging on the male. This is particularly so with the Chinese Hamster where the males are quite pronounced. Because of their small size, Russian and Roborovski Hamsters can be particularly difficult to sex for the inexperienced eye.

2 *The Right Start*

Thought should first be given as to where the hamster is to be located within the house. The cage should be placed in a room of constant temperature away from draughts and direct sunlight, and out of reach of any other pets which may bother the hamster.

It is always a good idea to buy the equipment and have the new home ready before buying the hamster so that it can be placed in the cage on your arrival home, keeping stress to a minimum.

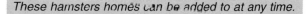

These hamsters homes can be added to at any time.

BASIC CAGES

There are various hamster cages sold in pet stores whose basic design consist of a plastic base and rigid wire top. These cages come in a variety of shapes, sizes and colours and are relatively cheap, easy to clean and long lasting.

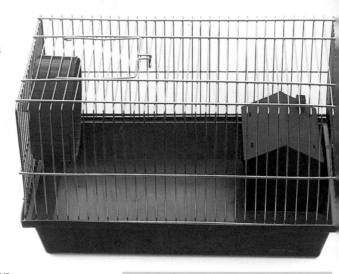

A basic hamster cage.

Because of their small size, cages of this type are unsuitable for Dwarf Hamsters. The bars are usually spaced too far apart and they can easily squeeze through and escape. There are, however, similar cages designed for mice where the bars are closer together, and these are more suitable for Dwarf Hamsters. Cages with high plastic bases will prevent wood shavings and food being kicked out of the cage by the hamster.

MULTI-LEVEL CAGES

Various multi-level cages are available – these may consist of a plastic base, rigid wire top and metal or plastic ladders leading up to another floor level within the cage. There are many different shapes and sizes of this type of cage today, some of which have some very nice features such as little bridges or climbing frames built into the cage. Some are very reasonably priced, although the more features it has, the more expensive the cage. These cages are long-lasting and relatively easy to clean. Again, cages with high bases will prevent wood shavings being kicked out of the cage by the hamster.

There are also several varieties of enclosed multi-level cages which have inter-connecting tubes and compartments. These cages are usually more expensive and can be difficult to clean, but are draught proof. They are not particularly suited to pregnant or very large

A multi-level wire cage, fitted with a wheel.

Syrian Hamsters, who may have difficulty moving through the inter-connecting tubes, but they are ideal for Dwarf Hamsters. The advantage of this type of cage is that extra compartments can be added to the cage at any time, enabling a bigger and better cage to be assembled as the hamster gets older.

AQUARIUMS

Various glass or plastic aquariums are available, and these make good cages for Syrian and Dwarf Hamsters alike. They are draught proof but glass aquariums can be cumbersome to clean out. Any top to the aquarium should be ventilated to avoid a build up of condensation. Aquariums are ideal cages for pregnant females, nursing mothers and baby hamsters.

HOME-MADE CAGES

Home-made cages can be constructed from wood and wire or from plastic storage containers and wire. Wooden cages will be gnawed by the hamster and will need constant repair. Cages built from plastic storage containers are draught proof and easy to clean, but do not allow the hamster to see out.

Whatever cage you buy for your hamster, you should always buy the biggest cage you can afford.

WOOD SHAVINGS

Wood shavings should be used to line the floor of the cage. Shavings rather than sawdust should be used, as fine sawdust can cause eye and nose irritations. In some countries, cedar shavings and pine shavings are sold for pets – pine is preferable to cedar which, while suitable for other pets, can cause irritation problems in hamsters due to the oil contained. It is always best to buy shavings from a pet store rather than from a lumberyard, where you cannot be

Shavings, paper bedding, food dish and drinking bottle.

sure that the wood has not been treated with some chemical which may be harmful to your hamster.

NESTING MATERIAL
Syrian Hamsters, particularly, will appreciate some nesting material – hay or shredded paper is best. Dwarf Hamsters will usually use shavings to make a nest but will also appreciate some bedding. Straw should not be used as this is sharp and can cause injury to the hamster's eyes or cheekpouches. There are a variety of manufactured bedding materials sold in pet stores. Man-made fibres and any material which is not easily broken or dissolved should not be used as it may cause

harm to the hamster if eaten, or if the hamster gets caught up in the material.

FOOD BOWL
Earthenware food bowls are preferable to plastic, which are easily knocked over and chewed by hamsters. However, hamsters will eat from the floor and this can provide extra stimulation, although it is easier to ensure your hamster is not overfed if a food bowl is used and refilled daily.

DRINKING BOTTLE
The best way to supply water for your hamster is by way of a drinking bottle. This ensures a good supply of clean water. Drinking bottles with a ball-bearing in the tube are best as these are less inclined to leak.

HAMSTER WHEELS
Many cages have wheels already fitted but, if not, it is possible to buy standalone wheels which can be placed inside any cage. Solid wheels are best, but runged wheels can have a strip of cardboard weaved through the rungs to avoid a hamster's feet slipping through. Some wheels may squeak after a while and this can be cured by placing a drop of vegetable oil

on the axle. Not all hamsters like to run on wheels, but for those that do it provides an excellent means of exercise.

HAMSTER BALLS

Many pet stores sell hamster balls, which are clear plastic with an opening in which the hamster can be placed. The ball can then be shut and the hamster can run, steering the ball around the house. These provide a safe way for hamsters to run around the house and prevent a loose hamster from diving under the sofa or other furniture, making capture difficult. Not all hamsters like hamster balls, and in any case a hamster should not be left in a ball for long periods of time. If your hamster does not enjoy using the ball, do not force it – find something else your hamster will enjoy. Balls are more suitable

A hamster ball provides good exercise, but for limited periods only

for Syrian Hamsters than for Dwarf Hamsters, who may have trouble pushing the ball around because of their small size. Once fully-grown most Dwarf Hamsters do seem to manage to push the balls around.

FURNISHING THE CAGE

The cage can be furnished with several items to provide additional stimulation for the hamster. Items sold in pet stores include plastic houses which provide a nesting place for the hamster (however, with a lid in place, condensation may build up in the summer and so it is best to remove the lid), hamster climbing blocks, hamster see-saws, tubes, etc. The cage may also be furnished with things such as toilet roll tubes, which the hamsters will use to tunnel in, as well as chew to pieces! Small branches of apple wood will also give the hamster something to climb on as well as to gnaw.

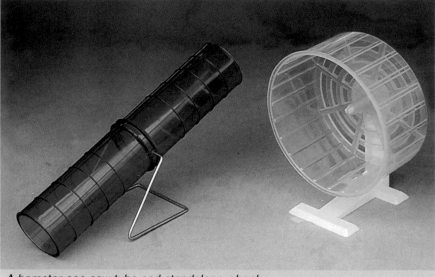

A hamster see-saw tube and standalone wheel.

PLAY AREAS

Many owners like to build their hamsters play areas and these can be easily made with simple, inexpensive items and some imagination. Aquariums or plastic storage boxes, filled three-quarters full with shavings or peat make excellent burrowing boxes and most hamsters love burrowing and tunnelling in these. Alternatively, aquariums or plastic storage boxes containing mazes, objects to climb on or tunnels also provide fun play areas for hamsters.

TRAVELLING BOXES

There may be occasions when it will be necessary to travel with your hamster, for example to the vet or to a show, and it may not be practicable to take the hamster in its cage. Small plastic pet carriers are available in most pet stores, and these provide an excellent way of transporting small pets.

FEEDING

Pre-prepared hamster mixes sold in pet stores are suitable for all types of hamster and should provide the correct dietary requirement for your hamster, and can be supplemented by a variety of treats. Do not buy foods designed for guinea pigs or rabbits, as these may not satisfy

A travelling box may be needed.

cereals, nuts and seeds such as crushed oats, barley, wheat, sunflower seeds, peanuts, maize, flaked peas and biscuit. Some mixes are not always of good quality, so look for a mix that has plenty of ingredients and an even quantity of each ingredient. If you buy your hamster from a breeder, find out what mix the hamster is used to and if possible, feed the same or a similar mix. If you wish to change the mix your hamster is fed, do

the dietary requirements of the hamster and may actually cause harm.

A hamster's stomach will not always digest all the required nutrients and so you may notice your hamster eating its own droppings. This is normal and nothing to worry about.

HAMSTER MIX

Basic hamster mixes sold in pet stores should form the main part of your hamster's diet. These hamster mixes consist of grains,

Pre-mixed hamster food should form the main part of the diet.

this gradually, feeding a little of both the old and new mixes at first, as a sudden change of diet could cause a stomach upset. Gradually increase the amount of the new mix and reduce the amount of the old mix over a few days, until feeding just the new mix.

GREEN FOOD

Most hamsters will appreciate some green food, although it is not necessary. Any green food should be introduced slowly to the diet, as too much too soon can cause diarrhoea. Most hamsters will normally eat carrot, cabbage, parsley, cauliflower leaves and stalks and apple. Although some hamsters will eat brussels sprouts and spinach, not all will appreciate them because of the strong taste. Most hamsters will eat lettuce, but too much can cause liver

Hamsters enjoy green food, but too much can lead to diarrhoea.

Clover.

Dandelion.

complaints. Dandelion, dock, groundsel, watercress and clover are also relished by most hamsters. Any green food should be clean, dry, pesticide-free and free from frost damage. Hamsters do have different tastes, and so not all hamsters will enjoy the same foods.

HAMSTER TREATS

There is a variety of hamster treats on sale in pet stores and most hamsters relish these. However, it should be remembered that any such treats are just that – treats, and should be fed as an occasional supplement to the hamster's basic diet. Some treats sold in pet stores are designed to be hung from the top of the cage – these provide stimulation as well as food for the hamster. Other treats that can be fed to your hamster are bread, scrambled or boiled egg, plain biscuit or cake. Never feed chocolate or toffee as these could cause the cheekpouches to become clogged.

Another treat appreciated by

Hamsters carry food in their cheekpouches – this cinnamon Syrian hamster has food in the left cheekpouch.

hamsters (but not always their owners) are mealworms. These can usually be found in pet stores that sell exotic pets such as snakes and tarantulas.

QUANTITY

Hamsters hoard their food and so overfeeding is not really a problem. The more a hamster is fed, the more food it will hoard, eating only what it needs. However, if too large a quantity of food is given, the hamster will pick out its favourite ingredients, which may be the fattening ones, so it is best not to feed too much. A handful of food each day is sufficient.

BRAN/OAT MASH

A bran or oat mash can be made with milk, porridge oats and bran, and hamsters will enjoy this as a supplement to their diet. This is a very good supplement for a pregnant female, a nursing mother and young hamsters. Muesli soaked in milk is also enjoyed by hamsters, as are some breakfast cereals (dry or in milk), but be careful not to feed too much sweetened food.

WATER

Clean water should always be available, and therefore it is important to ensure that the drinking bottle is never empty. Hamsters usually drink only 15-20 ml of water per day but may drink more in hot weather or less if green food is fed. Vitamin drops, which can be purchased in pet stores, can be added to the water to ensure that your hamster is receiving all the vitamins needed.

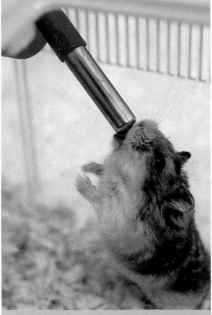

Clean water must be available at all times.

3 Caring For Your Hamster

The cage will need to be prepared by covering the cage floor with a good layer of wood shavings and placing a pile of bedding in one corner. However, the hamster is sure to move the bedding to another area of the cage! Fill the drinking bottle with water and fix it to the side of the cage at a height the hamster will be able to reach comfortably. Check by running your finger over the spout that water is getting through. Water bottles can be attached to aquariums by using self-adhesive Velcro pads, or some water bottles are designed to hang from wires which can be hooked over the top of the aquarium. Shallow aquariums with mesh tops can have water bottles fixed horizontally on to the top, but it should be borne in mind that the bottle will need refilling before it becomes half-empty. Place the food bowl and food in the cage,

Your hamster will need time to settle when it first arrives home.

and any other equipment such as a hamster wheel, hamster house, etc., and the cage is ready for its new occupant.

On arrival home with your new hamster, gently take it from the carrying box and place it in the cage. Your new hamster is sure to explore the cage, and start stuffing the bedding into its cheekpouches, and may take some time to decide on the location of its nest – only to change its mind and move it again. It is best to leave your new hamster in peace for the first day or two so that it has chance to become familiar with its new environment, smells and sounds and settle down into its new home. Speak gently when feeding your hamster, giving it the chance to become familiar with your voice.

If buying Dwarf Hamsters to live together, it is best to buy them at the same time – they need not be related but should be roughly the same size and age – and placed in their new home together. A watchful eye should be kept on them to ensure that no serious fighting occurs. There may

Russian Winter White hamsters.

be some squabbling as they get used to each other, and they will wish to establish an order of dominance. Unless serious injury is occurring it is best to leave them to sort this out without interference. If serious or prolonged fighting occurs, it may be necessary to separate them. However, often the squabbles are more vocal than physical and fights will sound worse than they are. Careful observation will indicate whether there is cause for concern.

GENERAL CARE

Your hamster is nocturnal, and so will sleep during the day and awaken in the evening. Therefore it is best to feed your hamster in the evening. By feeding a little earlier each evening it is possible to 'train' your hamster to awaken a little earlier. If you wish to waken your hamster at feeding time this is best done by tapping on the side of the cage – the hamster will take a while to wake fully. To poke a sleeping hamster usually results in only one outcome – a bite!

CLEANING THE CAGE

The cage should be cleaned once a

The cage should be cleaned once a week.

week, throwing away all the old wood shavings, hoarded food and any soiled bedding. Any clean bedding can be returned to the clean cage along with some fresh bedding. If it is necessary to wash the base of the cage, this can be done using a weak solution of washing-up liquid and water, rinsing thoroughly afterwards, or by using a disinfectant specifically designed for the cleaning of small animal cages. The water in the drinking bottle should be replaced with fresh water and the food dish refilled.

It may be necessary to remove any perishable foods from your hamster's food store between cage cleanings to avoid moist food becoming mouldy or starting to rot, so ensure green food is not hoarded or removed if placed in the food store.

Long-haired hamsters can be groomed with a soft toothbrush.

GROOMING

Hamsters do not require washing, as they wash themselves rather like a cat does – you will notice that your hamster will lick its paws or feet and then scratch or rub its coat.

Hamsters do not generally require grooming, although long-haired Syrian males may need to have the shavings removed from their coat from time to time. This is best done when handling your hamster, simply teasing the shavings from the coat with your fingers. If it is necessary to brush the coat, this is best done using an old soft toothbrush.

Dwarf Hamsters, particularly Dwarf Russian Hamsters, appreciate a dish filled with Chinchilla dust or sand which they use as a sand bath, rolling in the dust or sand to remove greasiness from the coat.

HANDLING YOUR HAMSTER

It may take a while for your hamster to become accustomed to being handled. Once your hamster has become used to its new surroundings, it is best to start handling by simply stroking the

Hamsters make good pets for children.

The correct way to hold a hamster.

As your hamster becomes more tame, he can walk from one hand to the other.

hamster while it is in its cage and talking to it gently, so that it has time to become familiar with you and your voice. Offer your hamster a food treat direct from your hand and give it the chance to smell you and get used to your scent.

Once your hamster is happy to be stroked in the cage, you can then begin to think about holding it. It is often easier to pick the hamster up if the top of the cage can be removed. You can then scoop your hamster up using both hands. Be careful not to lift your hamster too high as it may injure itself if it jumps. Always handle your hamster while sitting so that, should it jump, it will land in your lap. It is often better to ensure that the hamster is facing towards you rather than away when handling. This reduces the chance of the hamster falling on to the floor, and they seem less inclined to jump when facing this way.

Let the hamster walk from one hand to another and, should it try to jump, it is often better to let it than to try and hold on, which may frighten it – never squeeze your hamster. With gentle, regular handling, your hamster will become used to being handled in a short space of time.

RUNNING LOOSE

You may wish to let your hamster run loose during your periods of play, but this must always be done under supervision. Hamsters are quick movers and can run under furniture before you realise. Loose hamsters can also chew through electric cabling, furniture, squeeze through small gaps in furniture, etc., so a loose hamster may become lost or cause damage to furniture or to itself if left unsupervised.

Before letting your hamster run loose, you should also ensure that any other pets that may frighten or hurt the hamster are confined. It is not wise to let your hamster run loose outdoors as it could easily be harmed by other animals or birds (particularly birds of prey), and could easily escape or eat unsuitable plants which may be poisonous, fouled by other animals or treated with insecticides.

LEVELS OF RESPONSE

Your hamster will soon become accustomed to your voice and will show some response when you call its name. Rewarding particular actions with treats may enable you to 'train' your hamster to perform some of its natural actions. All

Standing and staring – the hamster's sense of hearing is acute.

hamsters are individuals, with their own characters, likes and dislikes.

ADDITIONAL CHECKS
Each time you clean the cage, check that your hamster's droppings appear normal – runny droppings may indicate diarrhoea, lack of droppings may indicate constipation. Check your hamster's teeth from time to time to ensure they are not broken or overgrowing. This can be done by carefully lifting the skin at the back of the neck to reveal the teeth at the front.

HAMSTER BEHAVIOUR

TEETH CHATTERING
This is a sign of annoyance and your hamster should be left alone at this time. Often, a hamster that

has been woken will chatter its teeth in annoyance and so you should leave handling your hamster until it has stopped. Handling a hamster that is chattering its teeth usually results in your being bitten.

STANDING AND STARING

The hamster stands on its hind legs with a vacant expression – something has caught your hamster's attention – it is listening intently to some sound. Hamsters' hearing is very acute and they can hear sounds beyond human hearing.

HIGH-PITCHED SCREAMING

Syrian Hamsters sometimes produce high-pitched screaming –

this is an expression of fear and will usually stop once your hamster becomes more confident. Speak to the hamster to reassure it.

Screaming in Russian Hamsters usually occurs during a confrontation between two hamsters and the submissive hamster will normally stand and scream at the dominant hamster, sometimes 'boxing' with its front paws or raising its paws in the air as if to say "OK, I give up – you are the boss!"

FIGHTING

Syrian Hamsters will fight if introduced to each other and serious injury can result. They are solitary by nature and should not

Gnawing will prevent the teeth growing too long.

be introduced to another hamster unless for breeding which, as explained later, should be carried out carefully.

Dwarf Hamsters, although social animals, will have occasional fights and these often sound much worse than they are and rarely result in any injury. These 'mock' or 'play' fights are common and are usually nothing to be alarmed about. Separation should only be considered if injury is evident, and it should be noted that, once separated, it may not be possible to re-introduce the hamsters to each other.

GNAWING

A hamster's teeth grow continuously and so it is necessary for your hamster to gnaw in order to prevent the teeth from overgrowing. There are wood chews, etc. sold in pet stores specifically for this purpose, but a hamster will also gnaw on hard dog biscuits, apple wood or the bars of its cage. It may also gnaw on the cage bars due to boredom.

SIDE RUBBING

Hamsters, particularly Syrian Hamsters, will sometimes rub their sides against areas of their cage. This is their way of marking their territory, laying down their scent from scent glands located on their hips, which may become sticky. These scent glands can be seen on the hips if the hair is parted and appear as raised bumps which may be pigmented with colour, looking almost like moles.

ESCAPES AND CAPTURES

Hamsters are good at escaping – give them a small gap and they will be out! They can flatten their bodies to squeeze through bars which you may think are too close together. Once out, they usually head for somewhere dark, such as under furniture. If your hamster escapes, ensure all outside doors are shut and ensure all other pets are kept out of the area.

Escaped hamsters do not usually travel far, and so there is always a good chance your hamster is still in the room in which the cage is located. Shut the door to confine the hamster to that room and search under the furniture. Hamsters also have an amazing ability to disappear! You can search the room from top to bottom and not find your hamster – but it will be there somewhere and so you may need to set a 'trap'.

The easiest and most effective

'trap' is to place a bucket or a waste paper basket in the middle of the room and place a ladder or build some steps outside the bucket so that your hamster will be able to climb up. Place some bedding and food in the bucket and leave the door to the room closed overnight. During the night your hamster should climb up the ladder or steps, fall into the bucket and be unable to get out again. By the morning you should find one sleeping hamster in the bottom of the bucket! Humane mouse traps can also be used to capture escaped Dwarf Hamsters, but are usually too small to use for escaped Syrian Hamsters.

Hamsters are great escape artists, so make sure the cage is secure.

4 *Species And Colours*

Over the years, many colour mutations have occurred and combining these mutant genes has created further colours. There are many different colours available today and some are listed below.

THE SYRIAN

COLOURS

The original wild colouring of the Syrian Hamster is the Golden. This is the most common of the colours seen in captivity and can vary in shade from light to dark Golden. Other common colours often seen in pet stores include Cinnamon, Black Eyed Cream, Red Eyed Cream, Sable, Mink, Dark Eared White and Flesh Eared White.

GOLDEN

The Golden is an 'agouti', that is, the belly colour is paler than the colour on the back, and the hamster has a dark cheekflash on each side of the face from the underside of the chin extending up towards the ear, bordered underneath by a pale crescent. The Golden has a golden brown coat and blowing on the fur will reveal a dark grey undercolour at the base of the coat. The belly is off-white and on each side of the face there is a black cheekflash bordered by an off-white crescent.

BLACK EYED CREAM

One of the early mutations discovered in 1951 is a 'self' coloured hamster; that is, it is the same colour all over with no markings. Self hamsters normally have a white stripe under the chin and can also have a white patch or spot on the chest or belly. For showing, there should be as little white as possible underneath on self coloured hamsters. The Black Eyed Cream has a rich sandy cream coat, black eyes and dark grey ears.

Red Eyed Cream: Note the dark red eyes and flesh ears

RED EYED CREAM

This is a self coloured hamster, peachy cream in colour, with red eyes and flesh coloured ears. The eyes of the Red Eyed Cream can be very dark red, almost ruby red in colour.

RUBY EYED CREAM

A very diluted cream, extremely rare and not to be confused with the more common Red Eyed Cream. The Ruby Eyed gene was discovered in 1948 and is believed extinct in the UK, although it may still be present in the USA. The Ruby Eyed gene can be combined with other colours to produce Ruby Eyed varieties of each colour, and has a strong diluting effect on the coat colour. Ruby Eyed males are normally sterile after 10 weeks of age.

CINNAMON

This attractive colour was discovered in 1958, an agouti, bright orange in colour with a blue/grey undercolour, brown cheekflashes, an ivory belly and crescents, red eyes and flesh coloured ears.

DARK EARED WHITE
Discovered in 1952, it is a pure white self coloured hamster with red eyes and dark grey ears.

FLESH EARED WHITE
Has the appearance of an albino, being white with red eyes and flesh coloured ears. However the Flesh Eared White is not a true albino but a synthetic albino, being bred from Dark Eared White and Cinnamon.

SABLE
A self coloured animal discovered in 1975 and once regarded as the black hamster although it is not jet black. It is often black when young, but lightens to a very dark brown or charcoal grey when older. It is easily distinguished by the cream colouring at the base of the hairs and the cream rings around the eyes, sometimes referred to as spectacles.

DARK GREY
An agouti discovered in 1964, it is a distinctive grey with dark grey undercolour, jet black cheekflashes, an ivory belly and crescents, dark grey ears and black eyes. Dark Greys are prone to spinal

Long Haired Flesh Eared White.

deformities and any Dark Grey showing a curled or kinked tail should not be bred from.

LIGHT GREY
A very rare agouti discovered in 1965. It is light grey in colour with distinctive cream colouring around the face, particularly the muzzle, and has a dark grey undercolour, dark grey cheekflashes, distinct cream crescents and a creamy ivory belly. The eyes are black and the ears dark grey.

SILVER GREY
A pale silvery grey with mid-grey undercolour, mid-grey cheekflashes, ivory belly and crescents, black eyes and grey ears. The face has an ivory tone.

BLONDE
Another rare agouti, a creamy blonde with light grey undercolour, brown/grey cheekflashes, and an ivory/cream belly and crescents. It has red eyes and flesh coloured ears and a distinct orange tinted muzzle.

Light Grey: Note the cream colouring around the face.

Long Haired Black Eyed Ivory.

BLACK EYED IVORY

A self coloured hamster, ivory in colour with black eyes and dark grey ears. Ivories can vary in tone, depending on breeding, being either a creamy ivory, a greyish ivory or an ivory with a pink tone.

RED EYED IVORY

A self coloured hamster, ivory in colour with red eyes and flesh coloured ears. The tone of the ivory coat can vary, as with the Black Eyed Ivory, depending on breeding.

BLACK

A self colour discovered in 1985/86, a jet black hamster with black eyes and dark grey ears. The Black usually has white 'socks'.

Black: This type often has white socks.

Mink hamsters brighten with age.

BEIGE
An agouti, pale brownish-grey in colour with a mid-grey undercolour, brown cheekflashes, ivory crescents and belly, black eyes and grey ears. It is rarely seen these days.

MINK
A self coloured hamster, brownish-orange in colour with flesh coloured ears and red eyes. Mink hamsters can be quite brown when young but may become brighter in colour as they age.

BLUE MINK
A self coloured hamster, mid-brown with a slight purple tone in colour, with flesh ears and red eyes.

CHOCOLATE (SABLE)
A self coloured hamster, the colour of milk chocolate with black eyes and dark grey ears.

CHOCOLATE (BLACK)
A self coloured hamster, the colour of dark chocolate with black eyes and dark grey ears.

DOVE

A self coloured hamster, dove brown in colour with red eyes and flesh coloured ears.

SMOKE PEARL

An agouti, a pale grey with an ivory undercolour, ivory belly and crescents. The cheekflashes are ticked grey and some of the hairs on the top coat have dark grey tips. The eyes are black and the ears are dark grey. Smoke Pearl is derived from Dark Grey and hence can also be prone to spinal deformities. Any Smoke Pearl with a curled or kinked tail should not be bred from.

LILAC

This is particularly attractive and is a lilac-grey agouti with a grey undercolour, ivory belly and crescents, grey/brown cheekflashes, red eyes and flesh coloured ears. Lilac is also derived from Dark Grey and hence can also be prone to spinal deformities. Any hamster showing such a deformity should not be bred from.

LILAC PEARL

An agouti, pale pink/grey in colour with the hairs ticked with grey at the tips, an ivory undercolour, pale grey cheekflashes, ivory crescents and belly, red eyes and flesh ears. Lilac Pearls are also prone to spinal deformities.

RUST

An agouti discovered in 1961, rust brown in colour, brown cheekflashes, ivory belly and crescents, black eyes and dark grey ears. It is fairly rare today.

COPPER

A self colour, bright copper in colour with red eyes and flesh coloured ears.

YELLOW

A sex linked gene combines with other colours to produce the female tortoiseshell, and was discovered in 1962. The Yellow is an agouti with a bright yellowish cream top coat, cream undercolour, and the tips of the hairs are dark grey/black. The cheekflashes are ticked black and the belly and crescents are ivory. The eyes are black and the ears dark grey.

HONEY

A soft orange agouti with a cream undercolour, darker orange cheekflashes, ivory belly and

Black Tortoiseshell and White.

crescents, red eyes and flesh coloured ears.

TORTOISESHELL

Produced using the sex linked Yellow. All Tortoiseshells are female. The Tortoiseshell is a bi-coloured animal, coloured with patches of yellow in the coat, ie. the Golden Tortoiseshell is Golden with varying amounts of yellow patches in the coat. By adding a white pattern, the Tortoiseshell and White is produced which is a tri-coloured animal. Tortoiseshells can be produced with most of the colours and the most striking of these must be the Black Tortoiseshell and White.

YELLOW BLACK

A very distinctive hamster. The yellow hairs are tipped with jet black to varying extents, the eyes are black and the ears dark grey.

UMBROUS

With an agouti colour this produces Umbrous Golden, Umbrous Cinnamon, etc. These have a 'sooty' appearance. For example, the Umbrous Golden is a dark golden with grey crescents and belly, almost as if the Golden Hamster has had a grey wash placed over its normal colour.

MOSAIC

A hamster of one colour often with a patch of another colour (usually black), for example a Black Eyed Cream with a jet black patch of colour. The patch of colour is usually on one side of the animal. Mosaics are 'freaks' and only crop up from time to time. Breeding from a Mosaic does not produce Mosaic offspring.

PATTERNS

Pattern mutations produce a white pattern which can be combined with any colour.

DOMINANT SPOT This pattern appeared in 1964. The hamster is predominantly white with spots of colouring. These spots can be of almost any colour and particularly attractive is the Black Dominant Spot Hamster. Some Dominant Spot Hamsters may have large patches of colour instead of spots and sometimes may not be obviously spotted at all, but all have a white blaze on the face and a white belly. The ideal Dominant Spot is one that is evenly and definitely spotted all over the back.

Cinnamon Dominant Spot

Blonde Banded.

BANDED was discovered in 1957 and has a white belly and a white band across the middle of the back. This white band can sometimes be incomplete, failing to meet in the middle of the back, or may contain spots of colour. The ideal Banded is one that has a complete white band taking up the middle third of the back.

ROAN is due to the White Bellied gene and is a particularly attractive hamster, being white with coloured hairs ticked through. These coloured hairs are often concentrated around the head, and the amount of colouring on the body can vary from hamster to hamster. Mating two Roans together or mating a Roan with a White Bellied Agouti produces eyeless Whites, which are white hamsters with very small black eyes or no eyes at all and so should therefore be avoided.

WHITE BELLIED gene combined with a self colour generally produces a Roan, and combined with an agouti colour produces a White Bellied colour, for example White Bellied Golden, where the belly is pure white instead of the normal ivory. Mating two White Bellied Hamsters together, or mating a Roan with a White Bellied Agouti, produces eyeless Whites. The white belly of a White Bellied Hamster should not be confused with the white belly on the Dominant Spot or Banded Hamsters. The Dominant Spot and Banded patterns have a white belly but this is not due to the White Bellied gene, and so mating Dominant Spots and Bandeds together will not produce eyeless white babies.

PIEBALD was discovered in 1948 and is now extinct in the UK. It is uncertain whether it exists in any country today. The Piebald is a white animal with coloured spots and patches on both the top coat and the belly, and not to be confused with the Dominant Spot, which has a pure white belly.

Long Haired Blue Mink Roan.

COAT TYPES

Over the years coat mutations have also appeared. These mutations affect the coat of the hamster and can be combined with any colour or pattern and with other coat types. For example, Short Haired Rex, Long Haired Satin, Long Haired Rex Satin, etc.

SHORT HAIRED is the normal wild coat.

LONG HAIRED appeared in 1972 and Long Haired Hamsters are sometimes referred to as Teddy Bear or Angora Hamsters in some countries. Long Haired females have a coat which is longer than the normal Short Haired, but is not spectacularly long. It is the males who can have the much longer coats, which can range from a few tufts around the rear end to long flowing coats all over.

REX appeared in 1970, and the hairs are lifted and slightly curled. This gives the coat a soft plush appearance in the Short Haired Hamster and a wavy coat in the Long Haired Hamster, with long haired males looking a little scruffy. The whiskers are curly.

SATIN was discovered in 1968 and gives the hamster a glossy coat. Satin mated to Satin produces double satinised

Long Haired Sable Rex.

hamsters, which have very thin coats and so should be avoided.

HAIRLESS was discovered prior to 1972 and is not widely kept.

Golden Satin.

However, Hairless Hamsters have been nicknamed Alien Hamsters in the USA and are sold on the pet market. The female Hairless Hamster can have problems producing milk for babies and so should not be bred from. The Hairless Hamster is not a variety which will appeal to all, and care should be taken with the breeding and distribution of offspring from Hairless Hamsters to avoid the gene becoming widespread and undetected in normal haired hamsters.

CAMPBELLS RUSSIAN HAMSTER

COLOURS

The normal colouring of the Campbells Russian is a brownish-grey top coat with a dark grey undercolour, a dark brown-grey dorsal stripe and ivory belly. There are three arches on the side separating the top colour and belly colour, and these arches have a rich creamy tint. The eyes are black and the ears are dark grey.

ALBINO was discovered in 1988 is pure white with red eyes and flesh ears.

ARGENTE was discovered in 1993/94 and is a bright rich orange with blue-grey undercolour, brown-grey dorsal stripe, red eyes and flesh coloured ears.

OPAL is a purple/blue-grey colour with a grey dorsal stripe and ivory belly, black eyes and grey ears.

BLACK EYED WHITE is white with black eyes and mottled ears, and occurs in litters from Platinums (see below). It is not a true Black Eyed White.

PATTERNS

The following pattern mutations

Albino Cambells Russian.

can be combined with any of the colour mutations listed above.

MOTTLED appeared in 1992 and is particularly attractive, being white with patches or spots of colour, or coloured with white patches or spots. The coloured parts are normal, Argente or Opal, for example normal Mottled, Argente Mottled, Opal Mottled. Mating Mottled to Mottled should be avoided, as this produces Black Eyed Whites which do not usually survive weaning.

Platinum Campbells Russian.

around the shoulders. It is possible to have Platinums in all colours, for example normal Platinum, Argente Platinum, Opal Platinum. Breeding Platinums can produce Black Eyed Whites, and these normally survive and are healthy.

COAT TYPES

SATIN appeared in 1981 and can be combined with any colour/pattern combination and gives the hamster a wet, greasy appearance. Albino Satins may look slightly yellow.

WAVY was discovered in 1992 and young hamsters have a slightly wavy coat and curly whiskers. The wavy coat however moults out

Mottled Campbells Russian.

PLATINUM appeared with the Mottled Hamster in 1992 and is another particularly attractive variety. The coat is ticked through with white hairs giving a silvering effect. Some Platinums may also have an intensity of white hairs after a few weeks leaving a normal coat but the curly whiskers remain. It is a rare mutation and often goes unnoticed.

WINTER WHITE RUSSIAN

COLOURS

The normal colouring is dark grey with almost black undercolour, a black dorsal stripe and ivory belly. There are three side arches separating the top colour from the belly colour, and the ivory areas under these arches are often ticked with grey hairs. The eyes are black and the ears are dark grey.

Winter White Russians are usually dark grey.

SAPPHIRE appeared in the 1980s and is a particularly attractive colour, having a purple-grey coat

Sapphire Winter White.

with grey dorsal stripe, black eyes and grey ears.

PATTERNS

PEARL discovered in 1988, is a white animal ticked through with coloured hairs. This ticking is often concentrated along the dorsal area. The normal Pearl has black ticking and the Sapphire Pearl has purple-grey ticking. The amount of ticking may vary from being mainly evident down the dorsal area to lightly ticked all over the back and heavily ticked along the dorsal area. Pearl males are generally sterile.

Dominant Spot Chinese.

CHINESE HAMSTERS

COLOURS

The normal colouring of the Chinese Hamster is a chestnut brown with black dorsal stripe and ivory belly, black eyes and grey ears.

BLACK EYED WHITE Chinese Hamsters sometimes occur in litters from Dominant Spots (see below). These are not actually a separate mutation but are Dominant Spots with no spots!

PATTERNS

DOMINANT SPOT appeared in 1981 and is white with patches of colour. The colouring tends to be slightly greyer than the normal brown colouring.

ROBOROVSKI HAMSTERS

COLOURS

The normal colouring is sandy golden with white belly and eyebrows, black eyes and flesh-coloured ears edged with grey. There are no colour mutations of the Roborovski at present.

Robrovski – there are no colour mutations as yet.

5 *Breeding Hamsters*

Many owners at some time or other decide that they would like to breed their hamsters. This may be because they want a baby hamster from their much-loved hamster; they may want a hamster ready to replace an elderly pet, or they may wish to make a profit from breeding hamsters.

MAKING THE DECISION

Firstly, breeding hamsters does not usually result in a profit. To breed hamsters, additional cages are needed and, for best litter results, Syrian Hamsters should not be bred from more than two or three times. Dwarf Hamsterswill breed more often, but they will often have smaller litters.

Secondly, before considering breeding you need to consider what you will do with the surplus babies. It should be borne in mind that the average litter for a Syrian Hamster is eight, although they can have up to 18 babies. The average litter for a Dwarf Campbells Russian is four to six, but up to 14 in one litter has been known. Dwarf Winter White Russians, Chinese and Roborovskis have an average of four to six babies but can have up to eight or nine. Dwarf Hamsters can have litters in quick succession, often three weeks apart, and so you could have periods where many babies are being produced.

Local pet stores may be willing to take or buy surplus babies from you, or you may have friends that would like to have a baby hamster from you. There may be a hamster show where you could sell some babies, but you should check this out before you breed your hamsters. Pet stores often have their own regular suppliers and are not willing to take one-off litters from pet owners. If they do, they will not pay a high price for the hamsters (usually only about a quarter or a third of the price that they sell them at in the store).

THE RIGHT AGE
A female Syrian Hamster can breed from as young as 21 days, but is best bred from for the first time at four to six months of age.

Male Russian hamster.

This gives the hamster time to mature, gain condition, and obtain full growth. To breed from a female younger than this could result in the female cannibalising or abandoning the litter, having difficulty producing milk or just bringing up a very poor litter due to her immaturity. Breeding at an early age can also stunt the growth of the female due to the strain put on her during her own development. Breeding a female for the first time at over six months of age can result in

Female Russian hamster.

difficulties giving birth and so is best avoided.

Once bred, the female should then be given three to four months to recover condition before breeding again at seven to ten months of age. Females are usually sterile at around 12 - 14 months of age.

Males can be used for breeding from as young as five weeks of age, but because of their small size at this age it is best left until they are a little older. Males are generally fertile for the majority of their life and some have been known to father litters at three-and-a-half years of age.

Dwarf Hamsters will usually start to breed at around three to four months of age, with the exception of the Roborovskis who are late developers and may not breed until they are eight months of age. Dwarf Hamsters normally regulate their breeding, and may have a few litters in quick succession and then have a 'rest period' where no breeding takes place.

Dwarf Winter White Russian Hamsters will not breed while in their winter coats, when their coat has lightened or turned white due to reduced daylight hours.

THE RIGHT CONDITION

Any hamster that is bred from or bought with breeding in mind should be of the highest quality and in good health. You may only be interested in breeding hamsters as pets and not for showing and so colour may be unimportant, but the size, condition and temperament of any hamster should be considered before breeding. Small, ill or under-conditioned hamsters should not be bred from and careful thought should be given to breeding from any hamster that has a bad temperament. Any hamster with a genetic deformity or any illness should not be bred from.

MATING

SYRIAN HAMSTERS

Syrian Hamsters are solitary animals and kept separately, so mating is not straightforward. The female will come into season or 'on heat' usually every four days although this can vary from between three and five days. Often

the female will emit a strong musky smell before coming into season, and will be noticeably more active when in season. As hamsters are nocturnal animals, females come into season in the evening and this may last through until the morning. In the winter, females may stop coming into season completely and this can be helped by leaving a light on during the day and evening and feeding greens - in short, trying to persuade the female that it is actually summer. In the middle of the summer females may not come into season until very late evening.

IN SEASON

A female, when in season, will 'freeze' or 'stand' - that is, she will stand completely still with her head pointing forward, stomach pressed to the ground and tail in the air, ready for the male to mate. Often a female will 'freeze' in this manner if her back is firmly stroked or if you attempt to pick her up. This is a good test to see if she is in season before putting her with a male.

If the female is suspected to be in season, she can be introduced to the male. They should be introduced on neutral territory or in the male's cage, but never in the female's cage as she will attack him even if she is in season and can cause the male serious injury.

If the female is in season she will 'freeze' when the male approaches and the male will lick and fuss the female and proceed to mount and dismount several times. Inexperienced males may take a little while to start mating or may attempt to mate from all angles, but generally they will understand what is required after a time! Some males can seem quite aggressive with the females, biting the loose skin of the female. They do not usually hurt the female when doing this, but if she appears to be annoyed they should be separated. The male and female should be allowed to mate for about 20 minutes, but if either hamster loses interest before that time they should be separated. Males do not always get the female pregnant first time and, if no pregnancy results, it may be necessary to do a repeat mating.

If the female is not in season when introduced to the male, fighting will usually occur and the female can cause serious injury to the male. They should be separated immediately if fighting breaks out and returned to their cages. The pair should be tried

Russian Winter Whites: Mating is much simpler between Dwarf hamsters.

again the following evening until the female is in season and mating takes place.

DWARF HAMSTERS
As Dwarf Hamsters live together in mixed sex pairs or groups, mating inevitably takes place when the hamsters are ready without any intervention from the owner. Often mating will not be seen.

PREGNANCY

SYRIAN HAMSTER
A pregnant hamster will often not come into season after a successful mating and this is the most obvious, but not always reliable, indication that a Syrian Hamster is pregnant. Four days after mating, try stroking the back of the female to see if she appears to be in season and 'freezes'. If she shows

no interest in mating she is probably pregnant. If she does 'freeze' introduce her once again to the male to see if she will accept a mating. If she does, it is likely that she was not pregnant but hopefully should be this time.

DWARF HAMSTERS
With Dwarf Hamsters, the first sign of pregnancy is often that the

A pregnant Syrian.

females become more aggressive towards the male. Pregnant females will often squabble with the males and may banish the males from the nest leading up to pregnancy or shortly after the birth.

THE PREGNANT HAMSTER

At around eight days after mating, the Syrian Hamster may begin to appear pregnant. Some may not appear to be pregnant until much later. Because of their small size, it is often more difficult to tell if Dwarf Hamsters are pregnant until a few days before the birth. The pregnant hamster should be fed plenty of food and a few treats, such as carrot, bread soaked in milk or scrambled egg. Vitamin drops in the water will also be beneficial at this time.

A pregnant female can become more aggressive and, if dropped or squeezed, injury can be done to the unborn babies or to the female and so careful handling is required. It is usually wise to keep handling to a minimum once pregnancy has started to show. It is often wise to remove the wheel during the latter part of pregnancy and while the mother is nursing, to avoid excessive exercise and neglect of the litter.

PREPARATIONS

You will need to consider the caging in which the female is to give birth. An aquarium is usually the best type of cage as this is draught proof. Also, the mother cannot accidentally kick the babies out of the cage, which can happen with normal hamster cages. Pregnant females may find the inter-connecting tubes of enclosed multi-level cages a bit of a squeeze, and any multi-level cage can result in babies injuring themselves falling, and so these are not ideal cages for a mother with babies. Also, as the babies grow and start to wander about, they can usually squeeze through the bars of a normal hamster cage.

The gestation period for the Syrian Hamster is 16 days, and so counting 16 days from the evening of mating will give the expected date of the arrival of the litter. Two days before this expected delivery date, the cage should be cleaned and plenty of nesting material provided so that the female can prepare herself for the birth. Plenty of food should be given.

The gestation period for Dwarf Russian Hamsters (Campbells and Winter Whites) and Chinese Hamsters is 18 - 21 days, and for

Roborovski Hamsters 23 - 30 days. As it is not always possible to determine the time of mating, it is not always possible to ensure the cage is cleaned a day or two before the birth. The cage should be kept reasonably clean at all times prior to the birth if any female is suspected to be pregnant.

THE BIRTH
The female will usually give birth during the evening or night and

Hamsters are born naked and blind – this litter is a day old.

Parents and babies – just a few hours old.

the babies are born at short intervals. The female may move around the cage while giving birth and may leave babies stranded in various corners of the cage. This is usually nothing to worry about as she will collect the babies together and take them to the nest once birthing is complete. There is likely to be some blood on the nesting material and this is quite normal and no cause for alarm. The babies are born without fur and are blind.

Female Dwarf Hamsters usually come into season soon after giving birth so beware, the male may mate again with the female shortly after the birth.

INSPECTING THE LITTER

You should resist the temptation to inspect the litter. The mother should be disturbed as little as possible, particularly during the first week. She should be given plenty of food, along with some bread soaked in milk and some healthy titbits. The babies are likely to be covered by the nesting material and so you may not be able to see them, but do not be tempted to disturb the nest to have a look as this is likely to upset the mother.

CARING FOR THE LITTER

The babies should not be touched for two weeks. If you touch them before this time you may change the scent of the babies and the mother may reject them. If it is necessary to pick up a baby, for example if one has been left out of the nest and the mother has not recovered it, this is best done with a spoon which has been wiped in some sawdust from the cage. The babies' skin will pigment if they are to be dark coloured hamsters at around three to six days and hair will begin to grow shortly afterwards. By two weeks of age they will be furred and their eyes will begin to open.

The babies will start to run

Dwarf hamster babies — the skin is starting to pigment.

Syrian: Ten days old: The hair has began to grow, but the eyes are still shut.

around the cage at around 10 - 14 days and the mother will usually retrieve them and take them back to the nest. The mother will pick the babies up in her mouth, often by the scruff of the neck but also by a leg or whatever she can get hold of to take them back to the nest. This is often met by vocal objections from the babies, but does not result in injury. At this time the mother may endlessly be collecting runaway babies, returning one to the nest only to find another baby has decided to explore its surroundings. It is no easy task bringing up a large litter! The babies will have started to eat solid food. Bread soaked in milk and scrambled or boiled egg will easily be eaten by the growing youngsters.

With Dwarf Hamsters, the male should not be removed from the cage during breeding or nursing as he plays a vital role in bringing up the babies. The female may banish him from the nest during the first few days after the birth, but will usually allow him to return after a while. He will contribute to the upbringing of the babies by

Sixteen days old: The hair is thicker and the eyes are open.

collecting food and keeping them warm while the mother is away from the nest. He will often collect food and bring it back to the nest for the female.

With colonies of Dwarf Hamsters where more than one female has a litter, they will often mix the litters in one nest and the mothers will take it in turns to nurse the litter. Any other females and the males in the colony may be banished from the nest for a few days but in time the males and remaining females will be allowed to return to the nest and will also help in looking after the babies. It is not uncommon to have a nest which contains litters of different ages within a colony.

WEANING
At three weeks of age the babies are fully weaned and can be removed from the mother and placed into a cage of their own. It is a good idea to remove the babies into two cages at this time – one for males and one for females to avoid breeding of brothers and sisters at such an early age. Again, care should be

Three weeks old: The babies are fully weaned.

taken over the choice of cage as the babies will squeeze though the bars of a typical hamster cage. Aquaria are ideal for baby hamsters, being draught-proof and escape-proof.

With Dwarf Hamsters, the mother may have given birth to another litter a couple of days before the first litter of babies are three weeks of age. Provided that the older babies are eating solid food without any problems and drinking from the water bottle, it is best to remove them at this time so that the mother can give her full attention to the new babies.

The babies should be given plenty of basic hamster food, together with continued feeding of bread soaked in milk (this is particularly so with Dwarf Hamsters that have been removed from the mother before three weeks of age due to the birth of another litter) and titbits such as

Six weeks old: Ready to go to their new homes.

carrots or scrambled or boiled egg. Do not however, feed too many vegetables as this could cause stomach upsets; a little every now and again is sufficient. This is the best time to start gently handling the babies and get them used to human contact.

At five weeks of age, the baby hamsters should be confident and happily accept being handled and are ready to go to new homes. They should not be given new homes before this time, as they need the contact of their littermates to avoid stress and to increase their confidence.

6 Showing Hamsters

The best way to start showing hamsters is to join a hamster, rodent or pet club. Some clubs have pages or sites on the Internet. Alternatively, your library, local pet store or friends who already have hamsters may be able to help you to locate a club.

A Yellow Satin Syrian: Hamsters shows are divided into classes for the different varieties.

Most Clubs hold regular shows and these will often consist of main classes for the more experienced exhibitors as well as pet classes, which are ideal for the first time exhibitor. The main classes usually consist of different classes for different colours and coat types, for example there may be a class for Short Haired Golden Hamsters, Long Haired Cream Hamsters etc., as well as classes for Dwarf Campbells Russians or Chinese Hamsters. Shows also usually have classes for Junior and Novice exhibitors.

In the main classes the hamsters are usually judged against written 'Standards'. These Standards may give a detailed description of the shape and build of the hamster (often referred to as 'type'), as well as colour Standards which set out the ideal colour and markings for hamsters for most of the colours available. The Standards also normally include guidance on size, condition, fur, eyes and ears.

In the pets classes, the hamsters are usually judged on overall tameness and condition and need not be of a particular colour or variety or fit particularly to the written Standards that apply to the main classes. You will often be able to speak to the judge afterwards and find out whether they think your hamster is of a good enough 'quality' to enter the main classes.

Clubs will normally notify their members of shows and details of how to enter, and the show rules that apply, in advance. They may also advertise locally in pet stores or local papers with details of forthcoming shows and how to enter your hamster.

GETTING READY

You may be required to enter your hamster in advance and clubs usually issue members with a show schedule (setting out the venue, time, classes and entry details) and an entry form. You should ensure that your hamster is in good condition and free from any illness or infection prior to entering it in to any show. Any hamsters that are ill are liable for disqualification and taking a hamster that is ill or out of condition to a show could cause the hamster to spread disease or illness among hamsters belonging to other exhibitors.

Many clubs require hamsters to be shown in special show pens, particularly if entering your hamster in the main classes, and if you don't have one of these you

If you are showing a longhaired hamster, it will need careful grooming.

may be able to hire one for the day from the club. Show pens are used to ensure that the owner of each hamster remains anonymous to the judge, provides the judge with an easy-to-open container to enable judging and limits the space needed for the hamsters to be displayed.

If you are entering your hamster in the pets class you may be able to show it in its own cage. You will need to check whether you are required to show your hamster in a show pen or its own cage beforehand and book a hire pen if required in advance. These details are normally given in the Show Schedule.

You should also ensure that you find out whether a particular floor covering should be used in the show pen or cage for showing. Long Haired hamsters in the main classes in the UK are shown on wood-based cat litter and Short

Haired hamsters and Dwarf Hamsters on wood shavings. Again, these details are normally included in the Show Schedule.

You should also check whether any items are required or not allowed in the show pen or cage. In the main classes in the UK, hamsters are required to have a piece of green food in the show pen as they will not have access to water during the day. Bedding and normal hamster mix are not allowed in the show pen. Hamsters entered in their own cage in the pets class are normally allowed all their normal accessories, bedding and food to remain in the cage.

AT THE SHOW

On the day of the show, check that your hamster appears well and clean. If your hamster appears unhappy or unwell on the day of the show it should not be taken as it could worsen your hamster's condition, spread illness at the show to hamsters belonging to other exhibitors and could be disqualified by the judge. Long Haired Syrian hamsters will need any shavings teased from their coat, and a brush with an old soft toothbrush. Any other hamster will not generally need grooming,

Longhaired hamsters are shown on wood-based cat litter.

but you may wish to just wipe your hamster's coat with a cloth.

If entering your hamster in the main class, prepare the show pen by placing a layer of wood-based cat litter (for Long Haired Syrian hamsters) or wood shavings (for Short Haired Syrian hamsters and Dwarf hamsters) in the show pen. Place a piece of vegetable in the show pen and finally, the hamster.

If you are entering your hamster in the pets class, you will need to prepare the cage by cleaning and placing clean wood shavings and bedding inside, replenishing food etc., and removing the water bottle for travelling. However, remember to take it with you to the show

Silver Grey Syrian: Each hamster is examined individually by the judge.

Ensure that you have everything you need for the show – a copy of the show schedule, a pen, some spare pieces of vegetables and, of course, your hamster and set off to the show, allowing plenty of time to arrive before judging is due to start. When travelling to the show it is a good idea to remove the water bottle from your hamster's cage as the motion of moving the cage, walking, or train or car movement will cause the bottle to drip and the cage floor to become wet. If you have a long journey to the show, place some cucumber or carrot in the cage to compensate for the hamster not having access to water during travelling.

On arrival at the show you should go to the Show Secretary, who will issue you with a show pen if you have hired one. The Show Secretary will issue you with a label with an identification number to stick on to your cage or show pen.

If showing your hamster in its cage, this label should be stuck to the side of the cage on the base and if showing in a show pen, the label is normally stuck on the top. You should make a note of the number on the pen label so that you can easily find your hamster at the end of a show – it is amazing how much alike several hamsters of the same colour can look when all placed in show pens and finding your own beloved pet among them may not be as easy as it sounds!

The Show Secretary will show you where to place your cage or show pen to await judging.

Long Haired Silver Roan Syrian.

Dove Dominant Spot Syrian: At the end of judging, a Best in Show is awarded.

JUDGING PROCEDURE

Whatever class your hamster is entered into, the judge will remove each hamster in turn from the show pen or cage in order to assess the hamster.

In the pets class, the judge will be looking for a well-conditioned animal with a nice temperament and will award each hamster marks accordingly before deciding on a winner.

In the 'main' classes, the judge will be looking for a hamster that is a good example of the colour, of good build, size and condition with good fur, and will judge the hamster according to Standards written for the variety or colour and then award marks.

The judge is usually helped by pen stewards. These are volunteers who will place the hamsters for each class on the judging table and then, once judged, place them back on the main tables in order of the marks given by the judge. Once one class has been judged, the pen stewards will collect the hamsters for the next class and place them on the judging table. Often clubs will welcome volunteers to act as pen stewards, so if you wish to learn more about judging and see how it is carried out, you should ask the Show Secretary if you could help with pen stewarding. There will usually be an experienced pen steward who will teach you and help you if it is your first time.

The judge is also assisted by a book steward who will note down the judge's marks and comments and total up the marks allocated to each hamster.

The judge will remove each hamster in turn and place it on a judging wire. This wire allows the judge to look at the hamster from all angles to assess its shape, build and quality of fur. As the judge considers the hamster against the written Standards, he/she will allocate marks and make comments about the hamster, and the book steward will fill in a judging form with the comments and marks given by the judge.

As each hamster is judged and awarded marks, they will be lined up on the judge's table in order, and at the end of each class the hamsters with the highest points will be awarded places. Clubs vary over the number of places they

award. The judge may use coloured stickers to indicate the hamsters that have been placed in each class, and these are stuck on the show pens once judging of the class is complete. At UK shows, these stickers are usually red for first, blue for second, yellow for third and green for fourth.

At the end of the show the Judge will award a Best In Show – this is the hamster that has the highest number of points awarded across all of the main classes.

During judging, exhibitors should not do anything that could indicate to the judge that they own a particular hamster. This could result in the hamster being disqualified.

Once judging has been completed, most judges will be happy to discuss any questions you may have about the judging of your hamster. If you wish to breed better hamsters, this is a good opportunity to find out what you should be aiming for in your breeding. However, the judge should not be disturbed while judging is taking place and so, if you do have any questions, you should wait until all judging is complete.

7 *Health Care*

Hamsters are quite hardy pets but some of the more common illnesses are listed below. If a hamster does become ill, because of their small size they can deteriorate quickly. If your hamster appears ill and does not improve within a couple of days, veterinary treatment should be sought as soon as possible.

COLDS

Hamsters can catch colds from humans and so, if you have a cold or 'flu, you should keep handling of your hamster to a minimum until you are recovered. A hamster with a cold will have a runny nose and will sneeze. The hamster should be kept in a warm room and if not recovered in a day or

The correct diet is a key factor in maintaining your hamster's health.

two, or if its condition worsens, should be taken to a vet.

DIARRHOEA

The most common cause of diarrhoea is overfeeding of green food. In the event of diarrhoea, you should cease feeding green food immediately, feeding only the basic hamster mix. If the hamster is not recovered in a day or two, it should be taken to a vet.

CONSTIPATION

Hamsters can suffer from constipation and the hamster may walk 'hunched up', as if in pain. There will be a lack of droppings in the cage. If constipation is suspected, feed some green food and, if there is no improvement within a day, take the hamster to a vet.

WET TAIL

Wet Tail is often confused with diarrhoea but is a totally different condition. Wet Tail is a bacterial infection, or imbalance of bacteria in the stomach, and can cause extreme diarrhoea, which is accompanied by a distinct unpleasant smell. The area around the anus of the hamster becomes sticky and wet-looking, and this can spread around the base of the

tail. The hamster often walks 'hunched up' as a result of being in pain and becomes listless. If Wet Tail is suspected veterinary advice should be taken immediately as this condition can be fatal. Any hamster with Wet Tail should be isolated from any other hamsters and you should wash your hands thoroughly after handling the infected animal to avoid passing the infection to any other hamster. If using a cage for a new hamster that was previously occupied by a hamster with Wet Tail, the cage should be thoroughly disinfected and left to stand for a few weeks before any new hamster is placed in it.

MITES

Occasionally hamsters may catch mites. These may be seen on the coat and may only be minor, in which case they can be treated with an anti-mite spray intended for birds or small animals and sold in pet stores. Care should be taken not to spray into the hamster's eyes. In severe cases of mites, veterinary advice should be sought immediately.

CUTS AND WOUNDS

Most cuts and wounds will heal by themselves, but serious wounds should be monitored and the hamster taken to a vet if any sign of infection occurs. Sometimes wounds can become infected resulting in an abscess.

HIBERNATION

This is not really an illness but older hamsters, particularly, can go into a state of hibernation if there is a sudden change in temperature. The hamster may appear dead, but if inspected closely, the whiskers will be seen to twitch. Any hibernating hamster should be aroused to avoid dehydration and

starvation. The hamster should be placed in a warm (but not hot) place, such as a warmer room, a coat pocket or held in your hands. Do not put the hamster by a radiator or fire.

As the hamster comes out of hibernation it may start to shake before waking. It may be some time before the hamster is fully awake, but once recovered the hamster should be given plenty of food and water should be available.

Hibernation does not usually affect Dwarf Hamsters, who

Campbells Russian Hamster.

withstand cold temperatures much better than Syrian Hamsters.

OVERGROWN/CHIPPED TEETH
As a hamster's teeth are continuously growing, there may occasionally be problems with the teeth overgrowing, or a chipped or broken tooth may result in the opposite tooth overgrowing. Overgrown teeth should be treated and a vet will be able to clip the teeth down to the correct length. Sometimes older hamsters may have a tooth that grows crooked, and this may result in the teeth overgrowing and may need regular clipping. You can attempt to do this yourself but it is best to get a vet to show you how and to watch you do it for the first time, to avoid cutting the hamster's tongue or cheek.

BROKEN LIMBS
Occasionally a hamster may fall

Smoke Pearl Syrian

Black tortiseshell and white dominant spot.

and break a limb. Unfortunately, because of their small size, there is nothing that can be done. It is not possible to put a plaster cast on a hamster's leg! However, the limb will heal itself given time although it may not heal straight, but this does not normally inconvenience the hamster. If a broken limb is suspected, remove the wheel from the cage and if possible place the hamster in an aquarium so that exercise is kept to a minimum. Feed some bread soaked in milk and let the limb heal naturally.

SHOCK

Sometimes a hamster may fall and become shocked, and may shiver or lie still, breathing heavily. Keep the hamster quiet and in the dark; cover the cage with a towel, or cup the hamster in your hands to screen out light. If the hamster is not recovered in a few minutes it may be necessary to take the hamster to the vet.

STROKES

Hamsters can suffer from strokes, although they usually occur in older hamsters. These most often happen at night and so the first sign is when, the following morning, the hamster is unbalanced and typically the head tilts to one side. The hamster may need help with feeding and drinking, but should recover sufficiently after a week or two. Hamsters who have suffered strokes may live quite a while longer and lead fairly normal lives, although some head tilt may remain.

FUR LOSS

Hamsters can lose fur around the hips and belly as they become older (usually over a year of age). This can be helped by sprinkling a crushed yeast tablet on the food every couple of days or adding vitamin drops to the food or water. Nursing females may also lose fur on the belly, although this will normally return once the litter is weaned.

Any fur loss accompanied by irritation, scratching, soreness, scabs or flakiness of skin should be checked out by a vet as it may be an indication of mites, an allergy or a skin infection.

BRAIN TUMOURS (WALTZING)

Sometimes (rarely) hamsters may develop a brain disorder which causes the hamster to continuously run in small circles. The symptoms usually occur at a young age (five to eight weeks) and the hamster is unable to run straight. These hamsters are sometimes referred to as 'Waltzing Hamsters' and, unfortunately, the disorder is untreatable, and so any hamster suffering a brain disorder should be humanely destroyed by a vet.

CANCERS/TUMOURS

Hamsters can suffer from cancers and tumours but these are often treatable. The hamster develops a hard lump which may increase in size rapidly. Early referral to a vet is vital to increase the chance of successful treatment.

LONG NAILS

Occasionally hamsters may develop long toenails and this can be helped by letting the hamster run on sandpaper, filing the nails down. Alternatively, a vet should be able to trim them. Dwarf Campbells Russian Hamsters do have longer nails than the other types of hamsters and this is normal. However, if the nails become so long that they start to curl under the feet, they will need to be clipped.

EYELESS HAMSTERS

Hamsters with very small or no eyes can occur if two hamsters containing the White Bellied (Roan) gene are bred together. These hamsters can lead a normal life as a hamster's eyesight is very poor and they rely mainly on smell and hearing.

LOSS OF LIMB

Sometimes a hamster may have a limb missing. This can be due to accident or genetic deformity. Most hamsters will manage perfectly adequately with one limb missing. Any hamster with a limb missing due to genetic deformity should not be bred from.

Dominant spot Chinese hamsters.